COMMON CENT$

THE COMPLETE MONEY MANAGEMENT WORKBOOK

COMMON CENTS

THE COMPLETE MONEY MANAGEMENT WORKBOOK

JUDY LAWRENCE

PUBLISHED BY DOW JONES-IRWIN
Homewood, Illinois 60430

ISBN   0-87094-694-3

Printed in the United States of America

1 2 3 4 5 6 7 8 9 0 ML 3 2 1 0 9 8 7 6

V

COMMON CENT$ is brilliantly designed to be your first vital step down the road to financial independence.

It provides you with a superbly organized workbook that enables you to account for each cent of your income. It then lets you plan for its disbursement according to your own priorities. By systematically completing each easy to use worksheet, you can obtain a firm grip on the best allocation of each of your dollars. It will not only reveal to you how your funds are being allocated, but will provide you with a precise time schedule for meeting each need.

I truly recommend this excellent workbook for anyone who is serious about getting their financial house in order.

Once you have accomplished this worthwhile objective, your next step should be to put your newly found investable dollars to work. My book, or other books by Certified Financial Planners can provide you with excellent guidance for accomplishing your goal of financial independence.

Venita VanCaspel
Author of the best seller
The Power of Money Dynamics

VI

DEDICATION

To my parents who inspired my skills and interest in managing money through their everyday example and to Linda for her emotional support.

Dear Reader,

There are hundreds of helpful money management books on the market, but people still tell me they just want a simple book to help them get their finances in order — a guideline that shows them and tells them in down-to-earth terms how to manage their money so they can get started immediately.

As a counselor, I originally designed this workbook for young families and women suddenly widowed or divorced who did not have money management skills and were often intimidated by the whole idea. I have since realized, through my workshops and the many letters from people of all professions and incomes, that managing finances is a universal concern.

Having money does not insure your ability to manage it. That's where this workbook comes in. It is written in easy-to-understand terms and is a complete, realistic, and comprehensive approach to managing your everyday money.

It is extremely gratifying to hear from so many of you since COMMON CENT$ first came out and to learn how this book has improved your lives.

I know you will appreciate the additional sections presented in this new edition. These new sections cover goals, needs/wants list, mail order records, and savings/ investment records.

If you are divorced and dealing with child support payments, you will be especially pleased to see the new section on child support records in the back.

I welcome your suggestions and comments to help me continually improve this workbook to fit your needs and help you reach your goals.

I look forward to hearing from you and wish you a successful and prosperous year.

Judy Lawrence

Judy Lawrence

I am grateful to many people for their help in putting together this new edition.

My special thanks goes to the following individuals who were supportive in the beginning when this book was in its first edition and who continued to give their support and encouragement as this book evolved into the current edition you now hold:

Dwight and Carol Myers for always being there, having the answers, and making good things happen.

Ken Wilson for creating the pleasing, non-intimidating visual effect of this book.

Ken Hoffmann for always following through and doing what he said he would do.

Janie Bluestein for giving her time, assistance and encouragement when they were needed the most.

Bonnie, Elsa, Bea and Cynthia for sharing their personal stories with me and sensitizing me to the needs of the divorced parent.

The many readers who have used this book year after year and whose suggestions are implemented in this new edition.

And especially my husband, Bill for his love, patience and support.

CONTENTS

An overview of the variety of worksheets available for getting maximum benefit from this workbook.

A place to write your goals and a method to help you stay on target for reaching those goals.

A guideline for paying the bills every month as well as for planning and organizing household and personal expenses.

A reminder of items or services each family member needs and/or wants when extra money is available.

A consolidated method for organizing and preparing for all the known and anticipated major expenses in a year's time.

A schedule for recording the cost and status of revolving charge accounts and loans.

A place to record all expenses charged to your credit cards. Helps you keep your spending under control and be better prepared when the bills arrive.

A method for keeping track of various mail order purchases so easily forgotten 30 to 60 days later.

A record of money earned and spent each month. Necessary when stablishing a personal budget and deciding which expenses need to be reduced.

CONTENTS

A summary of each month's total income and expenses. Good for measuring your financial progress and making future plans.

A record of mileage, dates, total bills, and reimbursements from insurance for visits to the doctor, hospital, drugstore etc. Necessary for tax and personal records.

Place to keep additional records needed for taxes or personal use such as auto, child care, education, casualty and theft losses.

A record of C.D.'s, money market accounts, stocks, bonds and other simple investments or savings.

A picture of your total financial worth. A valuable aid for loan and insurance purposes.

A place to record necessary information related to child support such as check number, amount, date, arrival date, etc.

A record of all necessary information if you ever need help from the Child Support Enforcement Agency.

A handy place to save bills, receipts, records and other important papers.

During these economic times, there is a great need for organizing and managing your spending. Whether you earn $50,000 a year or $5,000 a year it is important that you plan ahead and know where your money is going. The purpose of this money management workbook is to help you gain control of your finances — to know where your money is going and where it should be going.

Listed in the Table of Contents are the different work charts found in this book with an explanation of each. They provide a variety of methods to be used as guidelines for planning your own method of managing your money. Through these charts you will get a better overall picture of a month and a year at a glance.

How you use these charts depends on your own personal needs; how far in debt you may be; or just how out of touch you are with your finances. As one student put it, "It was after the bill collectors were knocking at my door that I realized I needed to use these charts and make them work for   me. Since I started using the Monthly Budget Work Sheet, I can plan and organize my spending so that the pay check actually lasts until the next one arrives. The charts will work, but you have to make them work."

Once you take the time and start planning with these charts, the results will be extremely rewarding. Whether you need better control of your money to keep the bill collectors from your door or to plan a trip to Hawaii, using the charts in this workbook will bring you closer to your goal.

3

THE PURPOSE OF THIS WORKBOOK

COMMON CENT$ is easy to understand and practical to use. Because it is flexible, it can be used immediately regardless of the time of year or condition of your finances. By following the guidelines in this workbook you will learn to take charge of your finances, instead of suddenly having to react to a crisis situation.

There are two purposes for this workbook. The first is to help you get your finances organized and keep proper records. With this workbook, you can keep records of your monthly expenses, medical costs, installment payments, credit card purchases, mail order purchases, child support payments, savings, investments and net worth information.

The second purpose is to help you plan and manage your finances. You can list and plan your goals; work out a method for paying your self, your bills, and your monthly expenses; remind yourself of items you need or want to buy when money is available; and plan ahead for the sporadic, but anticipated expenses throughout the year.

HOW TO GET STARTED

Set aside a block of time so you can thoroughly review the variety of sections available in this workbook. These sections contain instructions along with worksheets and charts which were designed to address many different needs. Each worksheet can be used independently or with another. Determine your own needs and see how this book will best fit them.

After reviewing this workbook, set up your own system for the next twelve months. Begin with the more permanent, one-time-only recording and planning sections. These will be more involved, but once they are completed you won't have to repeat the process. Then go on to the active planning and managing sections which will involve more daily and monthly participation.

WHICH SECTIONS TO COMPLETE FIRST

To complete the one-time-only section, gather up your checkbook register, bills and all other related household expense papers. Go to the **Yearly Budget Worksheet** page and read the instructions. Using the categories as a

4

guideline, determine your major anticipated yearly expenses and fill in the chart for the year with the amounts and the months due.

Next, turn to the **Installment Payment Record**. Go through your records and list those creditors being paid in installments. Fill in the "Payment Due" column straight across for the year. If some of your loans are paid off during the year, you will have a visual picture of when they will be paid. It will be easier to see how you can apply that extra money to your other loans. Also, by having a full picture of your debt status you will be less apt to over extend your credit, thus maintaining a good credit record.

Complete the **Savings/Investment Record** if this section applies to your financial situation. This section will require a great deal of detailed information, but it will be an invaluable record when it is completed.

The **Net Worth Statement** page is usually another once-a-year project unless you are updating the information for personal or loan purposes. Now that all your household papers are out, this is a good time to complete this chart.

The last section, but the most important, before going on to the day-to-day, money-management activities is **Setting Financial Goals**. Deciding on some of your goals at this time is very important. Be sure they are meaningful and important to you. Focusing on your goals will help you avoid discouragement or frustration and will motivate you to effectively manage your money.

MONTHLY INCOME AND EXPENSES

An important part of your monthly money management activities is knowing or finding out what your monthly income and expenses are. The **Monthly Expense Record** will help you find this out. You can either go back through your records and checkbook register, and by using the Monthly Expense Record as a guideline, reconstruct a month's worth of records. Or, you can start keeping records for a month and get a better idea of what your income is as well as learn what your general monthly expenses are.

JUST MINUTES A DAY

Your most time consuming task is finished. From here on, once you are in the habit of recording your expenses and other records (like mail order purchases or child support payments) and jotting down your needs/wants and goals ideas in this book, the process will soon become routine and take only minutes a day.

If both spouses spend money, each should remember what was spent and take a few minutes to record expenses on the **Monthly Expense Record**. The wealth of information you gain from those records will be worth the time you invest.

A FEW HOURS A MONTH

Bill-paying, whether it's once or twice a month, requires time to gather up your bills, checkbook, envelopes, stamps, etc. The **Monthly Budget Worksheet**, however, streamlines the whole process.

As you pay your bills and work out your monthly plan, refer to the following sections to help with your total planning: **Yearly Budget Worksheet** for any occasional bills due that month; the **Monthly Expense Record** showing the previous months' totals so you have a better estimate of food, gas and other general expenses; the **Installment Payment Record** for any loan payments due (be sure to record your payment and the balance due on this chart); and the **Credit Card Purchase Record** so you know how much of a bill to anticipate.

After an hour or two, you should have your bills paid and a clearer picture of where you stand for the current month as well as an idea for the next month.

PREPARE FOR THE EXPECTED AND UNEXPECTED

By setting up your system for the year, you are planning ahead and getting a full financial picture. As you plan ahead for your monthly budget it is important to remember to include three areas:

Reserve Account — After listing your predictable major anticipated yearly expenses on the Yearly Budget Worksheet such as car insurance, home improvement plans, tuition, gifts, etc., total these up. Divide this number by twelve to get the monthly amount you need to set aside in a bank or credit union for a reserve account (not emergency fund). This money will be for expenses you know will come up.

Enter this reserve account and amount on your Monthly Budget Worksheet under "Fixed Amounts" at the top of the page. When an annual insurance premium or tuition payment comes due you will be prepared and have the amount in the bank. These infrequent expenses will no longer disrupt your whole budget.

Emergency Account — There may also be times when unknown disasters come up. The hot water heater goes out or the car breaks down. Money needs to be set aside for the potential emergencies as well. Again, this account and whatever amount you put into the bank or credit union for it, should be entered on the Monthly Budget Worksheet under "Fixed Amounts"; at the top of the page. This money is *not* to be confused with the Reserve account which is actually being held for expenses that have already occurred.

Goals Account — An entire section of this workbook is devoted to identifying goals and saving for them. Goals are very important. This is the third area that should be included on your Monthly Budget Worksheet.

By including your Reserve, Emergency and Goals Accounts in the Monthly Budget Worksheet, you have a way of putting together and seeing your total financial picture. This process also reminds and encourages you to save and put funds aside regularly, offering you a system for staying in control of your finances.

WHO MANAGES THE FAMILY BUDGET

In most households, one spouse assumes the role "Family Budget Director" and stays with that role. This can, of course, be logical and efficient provided this person is good at managing money and enjoys doing so. However, it is very important that each spouse be involved with the household finances and responsibilities at some point even if they take on the responsibility every other year.

By getting involved with the family finances on some regular basis (every 6 months or year take over the responsibility from your spouse) you develop an awareness and understanding of your financial obligations, expenses, limitations, family spending patterns, and overall current financial status.

This awareness is important for personal relationships. If both spouses earn money, but occasionally the spouse managing the finances must announce that certain items or luxuries are not affordable, the news can bring up all kinds of bad feelings, confusion, and misunderstanding for the non-involved spouse. "Why not? We just were paid three days ago!" is not an uncommon response.

Without a total sense of the family finances it is difficult to know what you really can and cannot afford.

This awareness is especially important if there is ever an extended incapacitating illness, divorce or death in the family. When the spouse not familiar with the family finances suddenly is responsible for them, it can be a very frightening experience.

TAKE CHARGE OF YOUR LIFE AND MONEY

The methods and guidelines in this workbook will show you how to set your goals, watch your spending, and plan your expenses. You will then find that your bills are paid on time, more money is saved than you ever thought possible, your investments are off to a healthy start, your goals are being reached and the stress in your life is reduced.

As you take charge of your money, you will notice this control carry over to other aspects of your life. Your relationships with your family will become more relaxed and more time will be available to pay attention to other things in life besides just money.

Best of luck as you begin your new money management program!

6

Setting financial goals is one of the most important steps for gaining financial control. When you have a goal, you have the motivation needed to stick with a money management plan.

The worksheets on the next two pages will help you identify and record your financial goals and develop a plan for reaching them.

To begin, ask yourself what is important to you. What will make you happy and/or be a significant accomplishment? Define your goals in specific attainable terms (such as buying a red, two-door BMW instead of just a new car) and write them down. You have then taken the first step toward reaching your goals.

IMMEDIATE/SHORT RANGE GOALS

These goals are any that you have identified for the next month and/or year. Your goals depend on your interests and your lifestyle. Perhaps you want to save your Christmas money in advance this year, buy drapes, or pay off a major debt.

Do not forget your emergency fund. If you do not have at least three months take home pay set aside as a protection against unforeseen problems or disasters, this should be your *number one goal*. Once you have the security of knowing you are covered for possible emergencies, you can comfortably focus on your other goals.

When you reach the goals you have identified in this section you will have more confidence and discipline for the more aggressive goals in the Middle/Long Range Goals section.

MIDDLE/LONG RANGE GOALS

Middle Range goals are those you hope to reach 2 - 5 years from now. Maybe you are dreaming of a new home, starting a family, or trip abroad.

Long Range goals include plans beyond 5 years including retirement. By thinking about longer range periods you will make wiser use of your money. With time on your side, small amounts of money saved for 10 to 40 years will grow tremendously. And, if you pay closer attention to where you invest your money it will grow even more.

FAMILY AFFAIR

If you have a family, bring everyone together to discuss their interests and goals. Children need to take part in this activity not only to give their input, but to learn from the process for their own adult years.

There is seldom enough money to reach everyone's goals. When dad wants a boat, mom wants a piano and Junior wants a VCR, compromise is necessary. Each member of the family has to give and take and decide what is agreeable as a compromise. Rather than drop a major goal altogether, try delaying the deadline date.

FILLING IN YOUR IDENTIFIED GOALS WORKSHEET

Once you have defined your goals and written them down under "Goals", fill in the remainder of the chart. Number the "Priority" of each goal listed. Which goal do you want first, second, etc.? Which can wait a few months or another year?

What is your "Date Needed"? Six months, one year, six years? Every goal should have a beginning and ending date. Once you have committed yourself to a time frame in your mind and on paper, you have taken one more positive step towards reaching your goal.

"Cost Estimate" helps develop your estimating ability and forces you to do some research. By calling, reading or shopping to determine the estimated cost of buying a computer or putting in a pool, for example, your goal becomes more than just a dream.

If you have money in savings, how much of that "Amount Already Saved" do you want to use towards your goal? Write it down. Commit yourself to an amount.

"How to Achieve" is crucial. What are you willing to do to make your goal a reality? Will it involve working overtime, finding a second job? Will it mean trade-offs — cutting back or eliminating expenses like movies, meals out, or smoking — so you can reach your goal?

How much will you have to save each week, month, or year to reach your goals? If you have a difficult time setting aside money for your goals, arrange with your bank for direct deposit from your paycheck.

The Goals Savings Record Worksheet opposite the Identified Goals Worksheet is a great place for keeping track of your savings for your goals. Take your "Cost Estimate" figure and write it in the space next to "Total Cost". Divide that figure by twelve to see how much money you need to save every month. Each month record your savings and balance. You will be excited to actually see yourself coming closer to your goal each month.

PAY ATTENTION TO YOUR MONEY

If you have a strong desire for reaching your goal and you *really* want your money to work for you, you must pay attention to what you do with your money.

Earlier, I mentioned having time on your side and paying closer attention to your money. For long range goals (college, early retirement) where large amounts are necessary, these two factors are critical.

Let's say you decide to save $100 every month for ten years to reach your goal. You could stash that money under your favorite mattress and have $12,000 at the end of ten years. Obviously, that method is not the wisest or safest.

If you had chosen to take that monthly $100 to your bank and let it safely sit in a savings account and draw 5% compounded interest, after ten years you would have made nearly $5500 more "free" dollars for doing nothing more than driving over to your local bank. In the meantime, you would have saved $15,499 for your goal.

On the other hand, if you were to take time to find an account that gives 10% compounded interest for that same $100 every month for 10 years, your reward for your research time would be an extra $4653 over the 5% interest or an extra $8152 over the mattress investment, giving you $20,152 for your goal!

The more years you have to invest and the higher interest rate or return amount you get, the more money you will make. Look at financial books and magazines or talk to your local banker, broker, insurance agent, or financial planner, to examine your options. *When you learn how to effectively invest your hard earned money you can be confident you will reach your goals.*

IDENTIFIED GOALS WORKSHEET

IMMEDIATE/SHORT RANGE GOALS

Prio-rity	GOALS	Date Need	Cost Estim.	Amount Saved	How to Achieve ($ per month, 2nd Job, etc.)

MIDDLE/LONG RANGE GOALS

Prio-rity	GOALS	Date Need	Cost Estim.	Amount Saved	How to Achieve ($ per month, 2nd Job, etc.)

GOALS	Sample: IRA																
Total Cost	$2000.																
Monthly Deposit	$ 167.																
	Deposit	Balance	Deposit	Balance	Deposit	Balance	Deposit	Balance	Deposit	Balance	Deposit	Balance	Deposit	Balance	Deposit	Balance	Deposit	Balance
JANUARY	$167.	$167.																
FEBRUARY	167.	334.																
MARCH	150.	484.																
APRIL	160.	644.																
MAY	177.	821.																
JUNE	167.	988.																
JULY	157.	1145.																
AUGUST	177.	1322.																
SEPTEMBER	167.	1489.																
OCTOBER	167.	1656.																
NOVEMBER	177.	1833.																
DECEMBER	167.	2000.																
TOTAL	$2000.	$2000.																

9

Formula for determining monthly amount to save for each of your GOALS:

TOTAL COST OF YOUR GOAL ÷ NUMBER OF MONTHS left to date needed = AMOUNT PER MONTH need to save.

MONTHLY BUDGET WORK SHEET

WHY A MONTHLY BUDGET WORK SHEET?

The Monthly Budget Work Sheet is designed to provide a guideline for coordinating your monthly expenses with your take home pay. It is especially helpful during those lean times when the amount of bills you have to pay exceeds the money coming in. This method will give you a better overall picture of your monthly financial situation. The categories are kept general to allow for flexibility and necessary additions based on your own finances.

WHAT TO DO WITH THAT STACK OF BILLS

To use the Monthly Budget Work Sheet write the net amounts of each paycheck in the blanks at the top on the "Net Total Amount" line. You will notice the emphasis on Net Income and not on Gross Income throughout the book. This way you are dealing only with the cash you actually have for paying your bills. (See the Record Keeping Section for information regarding Payroll deductions and taxes.) How many columns under "checks" you fill in depends on how often you are paid each month. Of course there are many job situations where the amount may vary or is not always known such as sales commissions. If this is the case, make a very conservative estimate until the actual amount is known.

Under the check amount there is room to add the date each paycheck is received. This will help with your planning when working with due dates on the bills.

Secondly, divide the bills into two stacks: one for those that must be paid that month and another for those bills that can be postponed if necessary. Look at the amounts of the "must" bills and write their amounts in the appropriate blanks under the paychecks according to the due dates or other deadlines. At this point you may want or need to make arrangements ahead of time with the respective companies for partial or late payments for those bills you are unable to pay on time.

Try to distribute and balance the more expensive bills over the different pay periods rather than pay them all with one check. If you have enough money to handle more than the "must" bills, now is the time to distribute the amount of the "postponable" bills under the paychecks.

PAY YOURSELF FIRST

Notice that "Allowance" and "Savings" are under "Fixed Amounts". The phrase "Pay yourself first" has been said many times, but it is a valid statement and a very important rule because if you penny-pinch to the point where there is no money left for "Allowance", you will end up bickering, frustrated and disappointed with the whole budget idea. The "Allowance" should be yours to do with as you please. You need to decide how much "Allowance" each member needs in order to give flexibility for little splurges and yet not ignore the necessary expenses.

Just as important under "Fixed Amounts" is "Savings". Again, this is paying yourself first. You should consider "Savings" as an *expense*, setting aside a specific amount or percentage of your check at the same time you are completing the other categories of the work sheet. In this manner, you will be thinking of "Savings" as an expense so that it is planned for regularly and not dependent on leftover funds.

NOW FOR SOME PRACTICE AT BUDGETING

There will be many cases such as utilities or other areas under "Fixed Variable" and "Occasional" where the exact amount of the bill is unknown. For those categories a space for "Budget" has been included. This is where your budgeting practice comes in. This space can be used to help plan for the bills until the exact amount is known. Remember to keep in mind those other expenses that are not seen as bills but show up on a daily basis: (food, gas, entertainment, clothing, etc.) Those must be planned for as well. Here you will take an estimated guess (budget) as to what you will need and the amount you can spend. Once you become familiar with estimating your expenditures, you will start learning to live within your budget. If your budget is realistic, you will soon learn to do without certain unnecessary items in order to remain within the projected budget.

THE TIME FOR RE-EVALUATION

Finally, complete the "Totals" at the bottom of the page. After determining all the totals, you may have some columns that have more total bills than income and some columns that have more income than bills. Try to shuffle the bills to be paid to different columns so there will be a balance.

There may be some periods when no matter how much you shuffle the bills or postpone the bills to the last possible day, it is still impossible to pay them with only your pay check. This is the time for some real evaluation. You must decide what you need to change or do without in order to live within your income. Go over the budgeted expenses such as personal, clothing etc. to see if any of those costs can be postponed, cut back or eliminated. Contact the companies to make special payment arrangements. Many companies (utilities, doctors, department stores, etc.) are very willing to accommodate you if you will notify them and make partial payments.

In the meantime, possibly you have been building a small emergency fund and can cover expenses this time by withdrawing the necessary amount. This should be an absolute last resort, however, with cutbacks planned for the next month so you can gain control again.

GETTING CONTROL OF YOUR FINANCES

You have just completed an important step in getting and keeping control of your finances. Of course doing a Monthly Budget Work Sheet does not change or increase the amount of actual money earned. Being aware, however, of where and how the money is spent will give you the feeling that you are beginning to control your money, and help you stretch the use of those dollars more than before.

HAPPY BUDGETING!!!

MONTHLY BUDGET WORK SHEET

	Expenses	④ BUDGET	1st CHECK	2nd CHECK	3rd CHECK	4th CHECK
	① Net Total Amount		$388 | 25	$526 | 80	$388 | 25	$526 | 80
			Date: 10/10 ②	10/14	10/24	10/28
Fixed Amounts ③	Mortgage/Rent	$454 |				454 |
	Club/Dues	25 |			25 |	
	Car Payments (20th)	85 |		85 |		
	Other Loans Washer/Dryer	60 |	60 |			
	Insurance Prud.	64 | 30		64 | 30		
	Farm.	125 | 60		125 | 60		
	Savings	100 |	25 |	25 |	25 |	25 |
	Allowance Date Due:	100 |	25 |	25 |	25 |	25 |
Fixed Variable	Electricity (20th)	5,5 |		51 | 40		
	Gas/Fuel (12th)	15 |	13 | 79			
	Water/Garbage (21st)	17 |		15 | 98		
	Telephone (25th)	25 |			27 | 30	
	Gas/Auto/ Expense	125 |	25 |	25 |	75 |	
	Food	175 |	90 |		85 |	
	CHURCH	20 |		20 |		
Occasional	Personal	50 |		15 |		12 | 30
	Child Care Sitter	40 |			40 |	
	Household	45 |			30 |	
	Clothes	30 |				
	Medical	25 |		18 | 13	27 | 30	
	Misc. Presents	50 |			25 |	
	Subscription	15 |				13 | 45
Installment	Credit Cards M.C. (14th)	120 |	120 |			
	G.W. (16th)	25 | 43	25 | 43			
	B.W. (1st)	58 | 40		58 | 40		
	Total Expense		384 | 22	528 | 81	384 | 60	529 | 75
	Total Income		388 | 25	526 | 80	388 | 25	526 | 80
⑤	Total Excess		4 | 03		3 | 65	

January

MONTHLY BUDGET WORK SHEET

	Expenses	BUDGET	1st CHECK	2nd CHECK	3rd CHECK	4th CHECK
	Net Total Amount					
			Date:			
Fixed Amounts	Mortgage/Rent					
	Club/Dues					
	Car Payments					
	Other Loans					
	Insurance					
	Savings					
	Allowance					
Fixed Variable	Electricity					
	Gas/Fuel					
	Water/Garbage					
	Telephone					
	Gas/Auto/ Expense					
	Food					
Occasional	Personal					
	Child Care					
	Household					
	Clothes					
	Medical					
	Misc.					
Installment	Credit Cards					
	Total Expense					
	Total Income					
	Total Excess					
	Total Sheet					

February

MONTHLY BUDGET WORK SHEET

	Expenses	BUDGET	Date:	1st CHECK	2nd CHECK	3rd CHECK	4th CHECK
	Net Total Amount						
Fixed Amounts	Mortgage/Rent						
	Club/Dues						
	Car Payments						
	Other Loans						
	Insurance						
	Savings						
	Allowance						
Fixed Variable	Electricity						
	Gas/Fuel						
	Water/Garbage						
	Telephone						
	Gas/Auto/ Expense						
	Food						
Occasional	Personal						
	Child Care						
	Household						
	Clothes						
	Medical						
	Misc.						
Installment	Credit Cards						
	Total Expense						
	Total Income						
	Total Excess						

MONTHLY BUDGET WORK SHEET

			1st CHECK	2nd CHECK	3rd CHECK	4th CHECK
		Net Total Amount				
	Expenses	BUDGET	Date:			
Fixed Amounts	Mortgage/Rent					
	Club/Dues					
	Car Payments					
	Other Loans					
	Insurance					
	Savings					
	Allowance					
Fixed Variable	Electricity					
	Gas/Fuel					
	Water/Garbage					
	Telephone					
	Gas/Auto/ Expense					
	Food					
Occasional	Personal					
	Child Care					
	Household					
	Clothes					
	Medical					
	Misc.					
Installment	Credit Cards					
	Total Expense					
	Total Income					
	Total Excess					

April

MONTHLY BUDGET WORK SHEET

	Expenses	BUDGET	1st CHECK	2nd CHECK	3rd CHECK	4th CHECK
	Net Total Amount					
			Date:			
Fixed Amounts	Mortgage/Rent					
	Club/Dues					
	Car Payments					
	Other Loans					
	Insurance					
	Savings					
	Allowance					
Fixed Variable	Electricity					
	Gas/Fuel					
	Water/Garbage					
	Telephone					
	Gas/Auto/ Expense					
	Food					
Occasional	Personal					
	Child Care					
	Household					
	Clothes					
	Medical					
	Misc.					
Installment	Credit Cards					
	Total Expense					
	Total Income					
	Total Excess					

MONTHLY BUDGET WORK SHEET

	Expenses	BUDGET	1st CHECK	2nd CHECK	3rd CHECK	4th CHECK
	Net Total Amount		Date:			
Fixed Amounts	Mortgage/Rent					
	Club/Dues					
	Car Payments					
	Other Loans					
	Insurance					
	Savings					
	Allowance					
Fixed Variable	Electricity					
	Gas/Fuel					
	Water/Garbage					
	Telephone					
	Gas/Auto/ Expense					
	Food					
Occasional	Personal					
	Child Care					
	Household					
	Clothes					
	Medical					
	Misc.					
Installment	Credit Cards					
	Total Expense					
	Total Income					
	Total Excess					

June

MONTHLY BUDGET WORK SHEET

	Expenses	BUDGET	Date:	1st CHECK	2nd CHECK	3rd CHECK	4th CHECK
	Net Total Amount						
Fixed Amounts	Mortgage/Rent						
	Club/Dues						
	Car Payments						
	Other Loans						
	Insurance						
	Savings						
	Allowance						
Fixed Variable	Electricity						
	Gas/Fuel						
	Water/Garbage						
	Telephone						
	Gas/Auto/ Expense						
	Food						
Occasional	Personal						
	Child Care						
	Household						
	Clothes						
	Medical						
	Misc.						
Installment	Credit Cards						
	Total Expense						
	Total Income						
	Total Excess						

MONTHLY BUDGET WORK SHEET

		Net Total Amount		1st CHECK	2nd CHECK	3rd CHECK	4th CHECK
	Expenses	BUDGET	Date:				
Fixed Amounts	Mortgage/Rent						
	Club/Dues						
	Car Payments						
	Other Loans						
	Insurance						
	Savings						
	Allowance						
Fixed Variable	Electricity						
	Gas/Fuel						
	Water/Garbage						
	Telephone						
	Gas/Auto/ Expense						
	Food						
Occasional	Personal						
	Child Care						
	Household						
	Clothes						
	Medical						
	Misc.						
Installment	Credit Cards						
	Total Expense						
	Total Income						
	Total Excess						
	Total Short						

August

MONTHLY BUDGET WORK SHEET

		1st CHECK	2nd CHECK	3rd CHECK	4th CHECK
Net Total Amount					
Expenses	BUDGET	Date:			
Fixed Amounts — Mortgage/Rent					
Club/Dues					
Car Payments					
Other Loans					
Insurance					
Savings					
Allowance					
Fixed Variable — Electricity					
Gas/Fuel					
Water/Garbage					
Telephone					
Gas/Auto/ Expense					
Food					
Occasional — Personal					
Child Care					
Household					
Clothes					
Medical					
Misc.					
Installment — Credit Cards					
Total Expense					
Total Income					
Total Excess					

September

MONTHLY BUDGET WORK SHEET

	Expenses	BUDGET	1st CHECK	2nd CHECK	3rd CHECK	4th CHECK
	Net Total Amount					
			Date:			
Fixed Amounts	Mortgage/Rent					
	Club/Dues					
	Car Payments					
	Other Loans					
	Insurance					
	Savings					
	Allowance					
Fixed Variable	Electricity					
	Gas/Fuel					
	Water/Garbage					
	Telephone					
	Gas/Auto/ Expense					
	Food					
Occasional	Personal					
	Child Care					
	Household					
	Clothes					
	Medical					
	Misc.					
Installment	Credit Cards					
	Total Expense					
	Total Income					
	Total Excess					

October

MONTHLY BUDGET WORK SHEET

			1st CHECK	2nd CHECK	3rd CHECK	4th CHECK
	Net Total Amount					
	Expenses	BUDGET	Date:			
Fixed Amounts	Mortgage/Rent					
	Club/Dues					
	Car Payments					
	Other Loans					
	Insurance					
	Savings					
	Allowance					
Fixed Variable	Electricity					
	Gas/Fuel					
	Water/Garbage					
	Telephone					
	Gas/Auto/ Expense					
	Food					
Occasional	Personal					
	Child Care					
	Household					
	Clothes					
	Medical					
	Misc.					
Installment	Credit Cards					
	Total Expense					
	Total Income					
	Total Excess					

MONTHLY BUDGET WORK SHEET

	Expenses	BUDGET	1st CHECK	2nd CHECK	3rd CHECK	4th CHECK
	Net Total Amount					
			Date:			
Fixed Amounts	Mortgage/Rent					
	Club/Dues					
	Car Payments					
	Other Loans					
	Insurance					
	Savings					
	Allowance					
Fixed Variable	Electricity					
	Gas/Fuel					
	Water/Garbage					
	Telephone					
	Gas/Auto/ Expense					
	Food					
Occasional	Personal					
	Child Care					
	Household					
	Clothes					
	Medical					
	Misc.					
Installment	Credit Cards					
	Total Expense					
	Total Income					
	Total Excess					
	Total Short					

December

MONTHLY BUDGET WORK SHEET

	Expenses	BUDGET	1st CHECK Date:	2nd CHECK	3rd CHECK	4th CHECK
	Net Total Amount					
Fixed Amounts	Mortgage/Rent					
	Club/Dues					
	Car Payments					
	Other Loans					
	Insurance					
	Savings					
	Allowance					
Fixed Variable	Electricity					
	Gas/Fuel					
	Water/Garbage					
	Telephone					
	Gas/Auto/ Expense					
	Food					
Occasional	Personal					
	Child Care					
	Household					
	Clothes					
	Medical					
	Misc.					
Installment	Credit Cards					
	Total Expense					
	Total Income					
	Total Excess					

24

TAKING FURTHER CONTROL OF FINANCES

As you work with the Monthly Budget Worksheet you are making decisions about how you need and want to spend your monthly income. These decisions are an important step in getting and maintaining control of your finances and learning to live within your means.

This Needs/Wants List helps you take that control one step further. This section is designed to be a guideline for those times when you have extra money but want to be sure you don't waste it on things you really don't need or want.

NEEDS AND WANTS VERSUS GOALS

Needs, wants and goals as used in this book are all similar in that all are things you would like to have but must wait until you can afford them. With your improved budgeting skills and money awareness, you know you will have the capability to eventually acquire these items.

The difference between needs/wants and goals is primarily in cost and significance of the desired items. Goals, as presented in the earlier part of this book, are more significant plans involving time and gradual accumulation of funds for major purchases such as a stereo, car, or home. Elimination of a major debt is also a goal.

Needs and wants, on the other hand, are the smaller ticket items. These are the purchases made when extra money is left over after paying the bills and putting money aside for your savings and your goals.

HOW TO USE THIS LIST

Throughout the year you probably see or think about many things you need or would like to have, but don't have the extra cash at the time to buy them. Jot down all your ideas on this Needs/Wants List.

Items on your list can range from items seen in mail order catalogs, TV ads, or stores to activities such as going to a movie or new restaurant. Having these ideas written down will also make it easier for you to remember to watch for sales and list gift ideas as they come up.

At the same time, make a check mark either under the "Need" (necessities for your everyday well being like food, rent or medicine) or "Want" (which are nice to have, like albums, jewelry or theatre tickets, but which you can do without if you have to) column. This way you can make sure you take care of needs first when extra money is available. Record the source and cost of your items. When you are ready to purchase the listed item, the necessary information will be handy.

By using this Needs/Wants List you start establishing priorities and identifying what you really do want when you have extra money. When you have an extra $25 (which you determine after completing your Monthly Budget Worksheet) and a sale suddenly catches your eye, you won't be as apt to impulsively buy something. It will be easier to remember that there was something else you really wanted or needed when extra money is available.

A FAMILY AFFAIR

The ability to prioritize is a valuable skill for all age levels.

If your children ask for something when money is not available, write it down on the list. They will see you still care about their wants even if their desires can't be fulfilled immediately. In this way, children also learn to establish priorities and make choices. When money is available, they can choose which item(s) they want from their list.

PARENTS

CHILDREN

DATE	ITEM	NEED	WANT	SOURCE (store, catalog, other)	COST

DATE	ITEM	NEED	WANT	SOURCE (store, catalog, other)	COST

25

YEARLY BUDGET WORK SHEET
(MAJOR ANTICIPATED EXPENSES)

WHY A YEARLY BUDGET WORK SHEET?

The Yearly Budget Work Sheet is also provided as a guideline to be used alone or with any or all the other charts in this workbook. Your personal finances and method of handling them will determine which chart or charts to use and how to adapt them to your own household expenses.

While the Monthly Budget Work Sheet gives you a detailed picture of your monthly obligations, the Yearly Budget Work Sheet is designed to give you a general picture of your major yearly obligations at a glance, and can give you a more manageable picture than the use of files or notes on the calendar.

This is one more optional method to use for gaining control of your finances. It can prevent those periods when you may have had every bill figured just to the penny only to be deluged by the next day's mail with insurance or other bills you had overlooked or not anticipated.

When you have parts of the chart filled in (see sample) with all of your known anticipated major expenses you will see which months have fewer expenses than others. When you see that some months have quite a few expenses coming up you can plan to save a set amount ahead of time for those months, or try to arrange to change the due date to another month that has fewer expenses. For example, if your car insurance is due in March and September and both months already have life insurance premiums,and/or some other expenses due, contact the company and arrange to change the due months to May and November or whichever months are better.

You will notice that many lines are left blank in all categories. This allows room for you to add and change as many categories as necessary to fit your own financial situation.

FILLING IN YOUR YEARLY WORK SHEET

① **FIXED KNOWN** — Now the work and planning begins. This is the section where you will include those expenses you know are due and know their exact amounts. To determine your "Fixed Known" expenses such as insurance premiums, go through your policies, checkbook, or other records and find which months the premiums and other expenses are due. Premiums may be paid annually, semiannually or monthly. If your policies are monthly it may be more economical and convenient to change them to annual premiums. While doing this or when buying a new policy, look for the months that have the fewest expenses and arrange to change the due date to one of those months. While checking the policy amounts to enter on the chart, also jot down the policy number in the space provided. This will save you valuable time and effort in the future when you need to refer to those policies.

② **FIXED ESTIMATED** — In this section you will include all expenses you know will be due but do not know the exact amount. Including the utilities in this section may be more useful for some households than others. Some people arrange to pay averaged utility bills and others have fuel tanks filled at peak times so each situation will be different. For all cases, this section is helpful for record-keeping. When planning for the next year,the previous year's chart will show which months were high in utilities so you can budget accordingly.

The extra lines allow you to fill in your own fixed estimated expenses such as dues, school expenses, major hobbies etc.

③ **ESTIMATED** — This section will be especially helpful if you are on a very tight budget. Included here should be all those expenses that are not immediate and not essential but are preferred when the extra time and money are available.

Gifts for some households are minimal expenses; for others who place a high priority on gifts they can be a major expense when remembering Christmas, birthdays, weddings, Mother's and Father's day, anniversaries, baby showers etc.

Vacations can also be planned for in advance. Keep in mind the mini-weekend trip as well as those holiday and summer vacations. Fill in the amount you estimate it will cost and use that as a guideline. Both Gifts and Vacations are good places to learn to live within your income. You may enjoy buying expensive gifts or going on exotic vacations, but if it puts a hardship on your budget you may have to re-evaluate your priorities. Either spend less on those categories or less on some other categories.

Home Improvement expenses can range from a new mattress to an addition to the house. Included here or as a new category in the blank spaces would be hobby items such as new ski boots, additional items for a collection, etc. If you have been thinking about these expenses and trying to decide when you can afford them, use this Yearly Budget Work Sheet for your planning.

Credit is an optional category since an entire chart entitled "Installment Payment Record" is devoted to this. This section can be used for anticipated large bills or as a record. Here again you might consider listing the credit card numbers to save yourself valuable time in the event your credit cards are lost or stolen.

Major Medical and Major Auto expenses are some of those estimated expenses that are not only preferred but essential. You may not be able to wait and plan for that necessary major tuneup or set of tires under Major Auto Expense, or for those necessary eye glasses or dental work under Major Medical Expense. When those expenses come up you will have to rearrange or postpone some other planned expenses on the chart.If circumstances allow you to plan those expenses, however, this chart will help in scheduling them.

REMINDER

This chart is only a guideline and should be kept as flexible as possible. You are the one who decides how to fill in the blanks and which items to rearrange to make this chart work for you.

ARLY
DGET
ORK SHEET

MAJOR ANTICIPATED EXPENSES

YEAR 19___

Expenses	JAN.	FEB.	MAR.	APR.	MAY	JUNE	JULY	AUG.	SEPT.	OCT.	NOV.	DEC.	TOTAL
Mortgage/Rent	300	300	300	300	300	310	310	310	310	310	310	310	3670.00
Insurance: Life Prud.								144.90			64.90		209.80
COF			81.20						18.13				79.33
Autos H.M. – Car			98						98				196.00
H.M. – Truck					121.60						121.60		243.20
Health													
Retirement													
SPA	20	20	20	20	20	20	20	20	20	20	20	20	240.00
Electricity	30.98	32.20	23.30	29.67	20.30	30.10	45.20	40.04	43.30	29.10	30.00	29.40	383.59
Gas/Fuel	45.70	60.28	40.47	35.52	30.37	12.10	9.36	7.10	7.69	7.73	32.50	43.00	331.72
Water/Garbage	15.10	18.25	14.10	17.01	16.03	16.50	17.24	18.02	16.03	16.04	15.00	18.10	197.42
Phone	16.20	25.20	30.03	27.25	24.52	32.32	26.31	27.50	35.34	15.02	18.02	29.32	307.03
Gifts	20			10			50				300		380.00
Vacations						300							300
Major Medical Expenses										500			500
Major Auto Expenses		60					100						160
Home Improvement				500									500
Credit M.C.	360.50	110.67	300	250.30	320.10	310.40	100.60	98.60	405.10	89.10	165	210	2720.37
B.W.	15.20				25			18.59					58.79
G.W.		23.20				32.50					53		108.70
Total	822.98	649.80	800.90	1189.65	872.92	1063.92	688.71	734.20	960.94	984.99	655.95	959.82	9125.95

27

YEARLY BUDGET WORK SHEET

MAJOR ANTICIPATED EXPENSES

YEAR 19___

	Expenses	JAN.	FEB.	MAR.	APR.	MAY	JUNE	JULY	AUG.	SEPT.	OCT.	NOV.	DEC.	TOTAL
Fixed Known	Mortgage/Rent													
	Insurance: Life													
	Autos													
	Health													
	Retirement													
Fixed Estimated	Electricity													
	Gas/Fuel													
	Water/Garbage													
	Telephone													
Estimated	Gifts													
	Vacations													
	Major Medical Expenses													
	Major Auto Expenses													
	Home Improvement													
	Credit													
	Total													

WHEN TO USE THIS CHART

If you are beginning to get deep in debt or just need a better idea of how much you still owe on a medical bill or a car loan, this chart is an important part of your financial planning.

Rather than taking the long term payment bills that come in and stashing them in a drawer, hoping they will go away, and having no idea of the total amount you paid or the amount you still owe, start using this chart.

WHAT TO INCLUDE

The expenses you need to include on this chart are those that you are unable to pay in full and must extend over a long period of time. This chart will provide a better picture of how much you have paid, what you still owe, and how much it is costing you to pay in installments. (Remember every penny you pay for interest is money you could spend for something else.)

GETTING EXTRA MONEY

When you total the "Interest/Penalty Charges" column (the charge for paying late or in installments) at the end of the year, you will be amazed at the amount it has cost you!

By the following year, through the conscientious use of the charts in this book, you will no longer need this chart. At this point the total money usually spent on "Interest/Penalty Charges" will actually be extra money (savings) in your pocket.

GETTING CONTROL OF YOUR FINANCES

When you reach the point where you use credit to your advantage, and only as a means of using someone else's money, and can pay the bill in full when it is due, you will know you truly have control of your finances!

Rate	Creditors	JAN Payment Due	JAN Amount Paid	JAN Interest/Penalty	JAN Balance Due	FEB Payment Due	FEB Amount Paid	FEB Interest/Penalty	FEB Balance Due	MAR Payment Due	MAR Amount Paid	MAR Interest/Penalty	MAR Balance Due
	Credit Cards												
19.8%	AVCO VISA 14th /16		133			64	64	3,30 / 35.21	2133	129		34.54	2167
19.5%	Home Fed. VISA 4th	29	29	15.56	976	27	43	15.24	897				
19.8%	B of A VISA 10th		150		1946			5.00 / 30.77	1832	70		29.46	1762
15%	SDTCU VISA 9th	76	50	12.11	1281	74	76	15.98	1246				
X 21%	Crocker VISA 15th /16th		176		2985	88	88	51.40	2965	178		5 / 50.99	3021.31
	Loans												
X 17%	Central C.U. 25th	302.53	302.53			302.53	605.06		2555				
18%	Geo. Pacific 22th	104.03	∅		3411	104.03	208.06	60.56	3368				
15%	b.D. Teachers C.U. 1st	215	215	39.79	2948	215	215	37.56	2777				2588
	Crocker Prime line				11384		150	102.57	11289	102.57			11241
	Other (medical, legal etc.)												
X 21%	AX 1st Nationwide 9th	74		20.08	1063	74	100	22.59	1391				1414
	Total												

Rate	Creditors	APR Payment Due	APR Amount Paid	APR Interest/Penalty	APR Balance Due	MAY Payment Due	MAY Amount Paid	MAY Interest/Penalty	MAY Balance Due	JUN Payment Due	JUN Amount Paid
	Credit Cards										
19.8%	AVCO VISA 14th /16					121		32.57	2041		
19.5%	Home Fed. VISA 4th					52		13.88	882		
19.8%	B of A VISA 10th					67		27.85	1680		
15%	SDTCU VISA 9th				1377	183	183	18.33	1697		
X 21%	Crocker VISA 15th /16th					86		49.43	2879		
	Loans										
X 17%	Central C.U. 25th				1754						
18%	Geo. Pacific 22th				3244	104.03			3127		
15%	b.D. Teachers C.U. 1st	215	215	32.97	2406						
	Crocker Prime line				11209			10 / 97.84	11317		
	Other (medical, legal etc.)										
X 21%	AX 1st Nationwide 9th			23.33	1313				1335		
	Total										

30

$ 622.00 $ 871

		JULY				AUGUST				SEPTEMBER				OCTOBER				NOVEMBER				DECEMBER			
Interest/Penalty	Balance Due	Payment Due	Amount Paid	Interest/Penalty	Balance Due	Payment Due	Amount Paid	Interest/Penalty	Balance Due	Payment Due	Amount Paid	Interest/Penalty	Balance Due	Payment Due	Amount Paid	Interest/Penalty	Balance Due	Payment Due	Amount Paid	Interest/Penalty	Balance Due	Payment Due	Amount Paid	Interest/Penalty	Balance Due
22.54	1308																								

**CREDIT
CARD PURCHASE
RECORD**

To avoid a shocking bill at the end of the month, keep careful track of your cred card charges. This way you can anticipate what the billing will be and prepare for by making the appropriate adjustments in your spending and your planning.

By knowing the status of your charges at all times you become much more sele tive and careful about impulse charging. When you reach this point, you know yo have learned how to keep from getting over extended and have taken one mo step toward control over your finances.

32

JANUARY		FEBRUARY		MARCH		APRIL		MAY		JUNE	
Billing Cycle Closing Date: 1 _1-10-86_		American Xpress _2-10-86_		_________		_________		_________		_________	
Purchases	Amount	Purchases	Amount	Purchases	Amount	Purchases	Amount	Purchases	Amount	Purchases	Amount
3/ Gas 2	14 | 91	1/16 Air Fare	198 |	2/11 Air Fare	235 | 00						
7/ Shoes	20 | 82	1-31 Tapes	53 | 95								
		1-27 Tapes	53 |								
Total											

HOW TO USE THIS CHART

First find out and enter the Billing Cycle Closing Date. [1] Then record all charges made during the month [2] until that date so you know which purchases will be included in that month's upcoming bill. Purchases charged after that closing date should be entered in the next month's column (the month for which you will actually be billed.) Remember, this chart is flexible. If you use different cards frequently, then divide the monthly column into the necessary parts to keep the separate records. Make the chart work for you!

JULY		AUGUST		SEPTEMBER		OCTOBER		NOVEMBER		DECEMBER	
Purchases	Amount	Purchases	Amount	Purchases	Amount	Purchases	Amount	Purchases	Amount	Purchases	Amount

33

SHOPPING BY MAIL

Most mail or phone purchases are through ads found in catalogs, brochures, newspapers, magazines as well as TV and radio. There are advantages to shopping by mail including convenience and saving time. However, how many times have your ordered something by mail or phone (trusting it would arrive in 30 - 60 days), and it never arrived? Chances are you've had your share of mail order frustrations and undelivered orders (which you may have even forgotten) and now recognize the value of keeping records.

HOW TO KEEP RECORDS

If orders do not arrive as scheduled and follow up work is necessary, this Mail Order Purchase Record will be a valuable time- and money-saver for you.

Use this chart for all items ordered even if they are free. Log necessary information related to any purchases made by mail or phone. When you happen to remember an item you ordered some time ago and realize it still has not arrived, you can go back to your records, see when you ordered, then follow up by phone or mail, if necessary.

In some cases, it may be easier to cut out the ad with all the information given and tape it to the page, then fill in the "Amount Sent" and "How Paid" sections. If you order a list of items from a catalog, make a copy of the order form and save it in one of the pockets in back of this book. On the chart, make a note of the order, the catalog date and how you paid.

When placing a phone order be especially careful to record all the information on the chart, including the name of the person who took your order.

FTC MAIL ORDER RULE

The Federal Trade Commission's Mail Order Rule requires companies to ship an order within the time period mentioned in their advertisement. If no time period is mentioned, the company is required to ship an order within 30 days of receipt of your payment. The company must notify you if it cannot make the shipment within 30 days and send you an option notice of either consenting to a delay or canceling the order for a refund.

For a free brochure on the Mail Order Rule write Federal Trade Commission, 6th and Pennsylvania Avenue N.W. Washington D.C. 20580.

34

DATE ORDERED	ITEM(S) ORDERED (title, description, number, quantity, color)	SOURCE (magazine, TV, catalog)

COMPANY NAME / PHONE NUMBER	ADDRESS	PRICE	TOTAL SENT	HOW PAID (credit card, check no., money order, C.O.D.)	DATE RCVD.	FOLLOW UP NOTES (date called/wrote, contact person, action taken)

35

MONTHLY EXPENSE RECORD

With these charts and with some firm self-discipline, you will be able to keep a record of all money that you take in and spend each month. It will take some determination in the beginning to get into the habit of recording all expenses, but it will be worthwhile in the long run. You may want to begin by saving receipts and recording them daily or weekly, or you may rather just record expenses in a small notebook. The main idea is to get into the habit of recording expenses. The advantage of recording your expenses is the clear picture you get after a month that shows where you spend your money the most.

If you need to reduce or modify your spending and do not know where to begin, you will quickly see which optional expense categories you can start with. You may need to start doing more of your own home and car repairs, be more energy conscious, eat out less often, start car pooling, or whatever fits your abilities and interests. But when you do, you will notice the difference and the records you have kept will have paid off. There are twelve duplicate charts for you to keep up the recording of expenses each month.

You will notice the emphasis on Net Income throughout the book and not on Gross Income. The idea is to deal only with actual cash to work with and not record more information than you need to. The Gross Income information is always on your check stubs which you should save. If your situation is such that you need to keep a record of your taxes, FICA and other deductions, you can incorporate that information in the extra space provided under "Salary" on the Monthly Expense Record chart. A total of these deductions can then be recorded on the bottom of the Summary For the Year Chart.

SUMMARY FOR THE YEAR RECORD

The totals you have at the end of each month in the Monthly Expense Record chart should be transferred to this chart so you will have a total picture. This Summary for the Year Record is an excellent chart for measuring your financial progress and setting your future goals.

MEDICAL EXPENSE RECORDS

If you need to keep additional records on medical expenses you can use the chart following the Summary chart. A space is provided for mileage which at this writing is tax deductible. The column for Insurance Reimbursements is provided for those households that must pay the medical bill first before submitting a claim or pay the difference that wasn't covered by insurance. There too, the total amount you paid and the amount the insurance paid will be helpful when figuring your taxes.

MISCELLANEOUS EXPENSE RECORDS

Additional charts with the title space left blank are provided for records of other expenses, such as car expenses, child care, etc.

HAVE A SUCCESSFUL YEAR!!

38

Net Income

	Husband	Wife	TOTAL
SALARY	426.80	383.25	810.05
	426.80	383.25	810.05
Insurance Reimburse.		20.10	20.10
Dividend		10.20	10.20
Flea Mkt.		35.00	35.00
TOTAL INCOME			1684.70

Savings

(Describe)	
House Fund	50.00
Trip Fund	60.00
Emergency Fund	100.00
TOTAL SAVINGS	210.00

Investments

(Describe)	
Stock	93.00
TOTAL INVESTMENTS	93.00

Retirement

(Describe)	
TOTAL RETIREMENT	

	Food		Household			Transportation			Personal		Recreation		
	groceries	meals out	supplies, mainten	appliance furniture, furnishing	misc.	gas	auto mainten.	transit, tolls parking	clothing, sewing	health, beauty aids	vacation trips	entertain. clubs	hobbi[es] lesso[ns]
1	2.30					12.50						30.00	
2	13.76		15.00				45.00			6.00			
3	12.31	5.02		15.00		6.00		1.00					10.4
4	1.46									12.00			
5	25.15		1.38									5.75	
6	5.03					11.75							
7		20.45					24.00						
8	2.93					8.70		.50					
9			2.30						15.25				
10	1.75					10.95						7.00	
11		2.54					2.06						
12	7.40												
13	20.35		.68			13.20							
14													
15													
16	5.42					6.70							
17									45.00				
18	2.95												
19	3.70												
20													
21	16.43												
22													
23													
24	20.40												
25													
26													
27	10.90												
28													
29													
30													
31													
Total Spent	152.24	28.01	19.36	15.00	—	68.80	71.06	1.50	27.25	51.00	—	42.75	10.4

Education		Miscellaneous			Tax Deductible Expenses					
tuition, supplies	books, maga-zines	gifts, cards	other	other Cat	interest, taxes	medical	contribut.	business education	childcare	explanation
	4.55									
				10.00		12.40				
		2.40								
								25.00		wk. shop
				3.00						
						4.00			9.00	
	.55			2.00						
						45.20				
		10.50								
10.40									4.00	
				2.20						
—	15.50	12.90	—	17.30	—	61.60	—	25.00	7.00	

Fixed Expenses	
MONTHLY	AMOUNT
Mortgage/Rent	300 00
Gas/Fuel	31 23
Electricity	33 45
Water	19 00
Garbage	
Telephone	21 32
TOTAL	405 00
PERIODIC	
Insurance:	
House/Apt	
Auto H.m – Truck	125 00
Life Prud.	64 00
Health	
TOTAL	
INSTALLMENT	
Loans/Credit Cards/etc.	
Truck	75 00
m.c.	50 40
B.W. Dept. Store	35 30
TOTAL	160 70
GRAND TOTAL — Columns Above	754 70
Columns at Left	619 02
Total	1373 72

40

Net Income

	Husband	Wife	TOTAL
SALARY			
TOTAL INCOME			

Savings

(Describe)	
TOTAL SAVINGS	

Investments

(Describe)	
TOTAL INVESTMENTS	

Retirement

(Describe)	
TOTAL RETIREMENT	

	Food		Household			Transportation			Personal		Recreation		
	groceries	meals out	supplies, mainten	appliance, furniture, furnishing	misc.	gas	auto mainten.	transit, tolls parking	clothing, sewing	health, beauty aids	vacation trips	entertain. clubs	hobbies lessons
1													
2													
3													
4													
5													
6													
7													
8													
9													
10													
11													
12													
13													
14													
15													
16													
17													
18													
19													
20													
21													
22													
23													
24													
25													
26													
27													
28													
29													
30													
31													
Total Spent													

41

Education		Miscellaneous			Tax Deductible Expenses					
tuition, supplies	books, maga-zines	gifts, cards	other	other	interest, taxes	medical	contri-butions	business education	childcare	explanation

	Fixed Expenses	
	MONTHLY	AMOUNT
1	Mortgage/ Rent	
2	Gas/Fuel	
3	Electricity	
4	Water	
5	Garbage	
6	Telephone	
7		
8		
9		
10	TOTAL	
11	PERIODIC	
12		
13	Insurance:	
14	House/Apt	
15	Auto	
16	Life	
17	Health	
18		
19	TOTAL	
20	INSTALLMENT	
21		
22	Loans/Credit Cards/etc.	
23		
24		
25		
26		
27		
28		
29		
30	TOTAL	
31		
GRAND TOTAL	Columns Above	
	Columns at Left	
	Total	

42

Net Income

	Husband	Wife	TOTAL
SALARY			
TOTAL INCOME			

Savings

(Describe)	
TOTAL SAVINGS	

Investments

(Describe)	
TOTAL INVESTMENTS	

Retirement

(Describe)	
TOTAL RETIREMENT	

	Food		Household			Transportation			Personal		Recreation		
	groceries	meals out	supplies, mainten	appliance furniture, furnishing	misc.	gas	auto mainten.	transit, tolls parking	clothing, sewing	health, beauty aids	vacation trips	entertain. clubs	hobbi lesso
1													
2													
3													
4													
5													
6													
7													
8													
9													
10													
11													
12													
13													
14													
15													
16													
17													
18													
19													
20													
21													
22													
23													
24													
25													
26													
27													
28													
29													
30													
31													
Total Spent													

Education		Miscellaneous			Tax Deductible Expenses					
tion, pplies	books, maga-zines	gifts, cards	other	other	interest, taxes	medical	contri-butions	business education	childcare	explanation

Fixed Expenses

	MONTHLY	AMOUNT
1	Mortgage/ Rent	
2	Gas/Fuel	
3	Electricity	
4	Water	
5	Garbage	
6	Telephone	
7		
8		
9		
10	TOTAL	

	PERIODIC	
11		
12		
13	Insurance:	
14	House/Apt	
15	Auto	
16	Life	
17	Health	
18		
19	TOTAL	

	INSTALLMENT	
20		
21		
22	Loans/Credit Cards/etc.	
23		
24		
25		
26		
27		
28		
29		
30	TOTAL	
31		

GRAND TOTAL	Columns Above	
	Columns at Left	
	Total	

MONTHLY EXPENSE RECORD

Net Income

	Husband	Wife	TOTAL
SALARY			
TOTAL INCOME			

Savings

(Describe)	
TOTAL SAVINGS	

Investments

(Describe)	
TOTAL INVESTMENTS	

Retirement

(Describe)	
TOTAL RETIREMENT	

	Food		Household			Transportation			Personal		Recreation		
	groceries	meals out	supplies, mainten	appliance furniture, furnishing	misc.	gas	auto mainten.	transit, tolls parking	clothing, sewing	health, beauty aids	vacation trips	entertain. clubs	hobbi lesso
1													
2													
3													
4													
5													
6													
7													
8													
9													
10													
11													
12													
13													
14													
15													
16													
17													
18													
19													
20													
21													
22													
23													
24													
25													
26													
27													
28													
29													
30													
31													
Total Spent													

March

Education		Miscellaneous			Tax Deductible Expenses					
tion, pplies	books, maga-zines	gifts, cards	other	other	interest, taxes	medical	contri-butions	business education	childcare	explanation

Fixed Expenses

	MONTHLY	AMOUNT
1	Mortgage/ Rent	
2	Gas/Fuel	
3	Electricity	
4	Water	
5	Garbage	
6	Telephone	
7		
8		
9		
10	TOTAL	
11	PERIODIC	
12		
13	Insurance:	
14	House/Apt	
15	Auto	
16	Life	
17	Health	
18		
19	TOTAL	
20	INSTALLMENT	
21		
22	Loans/Credit Cards/etc.	
23		
24		
25		
26		
27		
28		
29		
30	TOTAL	
31		
GRAND TOTAL	Columns Above	
	Columns at Left	
	Total	

45

46

Net Income

	Husband	Wife	TOTAL
SALARY			
TOTAL INCOME			

Savings

(Describe)		
TOTAL SAVINGS		

Investments

(Describe)		
TOTAL INVESTMENTS		

Retirement

(Describe)		
TOTAL RETIREMENT		

	Food		Household			Transportation			Personal		Recreation		
	groceries	meals out	supplies, mainten	appliance furniture, furnishing	misc.	gas	auto mainten.	transit, tolls parking	clothing, sewing	health, beauty aids	vacation trips	entertain. clubs	hobbie lessor
1													
2													
3													
4													
5													
6													
7													
8													
9													
10													
11													
12													
13													
14													
15													
16													
17													
18													
19													
20													
21													
22													
23													
24													
25													
26													
27													
28													
29													
30													
31													
Total Spent													

April

Education | Miscellaneous | Tax Deductible Expenses

tuition, supplies	books, maga-zines	gifts, cards	other	other	interest, taxes	medical	contri-butions	business education	childcare	explanation

Fixed Expenses

	MONTHLY	AMOUNT
1	Mortgage/ Rent	
2	Gas/Fuel	
3	Electricity	
4	Water	
5	Garbage	
6	Telephone	
7		
8		
9		
10	TOTAL	

	PERIODIC	
11		
12		
13	Insurance:	
14	House/Apt	
15	Auto	
16	Life	
17	Health	
18		
19	TOTAL	

	INSTALLMENT	
20		
21		
22	Loans/Credit Cards/etc.	
23		
24		
25		
26		
27		
28		
29		
30	TOTAL	
31		

GRAND TOTAL	Columns Above	
	Columns at Left	
	Total	

48

Net Income

	Husband	Wife	TOTAL
SALARY			
TOTAL INCOME			

Savings

(Describe)	
TOTAL SAVINGS	

Investments

(Describe)	
TOTAL INVESTMENTS	

Retirement

(Describe)	
TOTAL RETIREMENT	

	Food		Household			Transportation			Personal		Recreation		
	groceries	meals out	supplies, mainten	appliance furniture, furnishing	misc.	gas	auto mainten.	transit, tolls parking	clothing, sewing	health, beauty aids	vacation trips	entertain. clubs	hobbies lessons
1													
2													
3													
4													
5													
6													
7													
8													
9													
10													
11													
12													
13													
14													
15													
16													
17													
18													
19													
20													
21													
22													
23													
24													
25													
26													
27													
28													
29													
30													
31													
Total Spent													

May

49

Left table

Education		Miscellaneous			Tax Deductible Expenses					
tion, pplies	books, maga-zines	gifts, cards	other	other	interest, taxes	medical	contri-butions	business education	childcare	explanation

Fixed Expenses

	MONTHLY	AMOUNT
1	Mortgage/ Rent	
2	Gas/Fuel	
3	Electricity	
4	Water	
5	Garbage	
6	Telephone	
7		
8		
9		
10	TOTAL	
11	**PERIODIC**	
12		
13	Insurance:	
14	House/Apt	
15	Auto	
16	Life	
17	Health	
18		
19	TOTAL	
20	**INSTALLMENT**	
21		
22	Loans/Credit Cards/etc.	
23		
24		
25		
26		
27		
28		
29		
30	TOTAL	
31		
GRAND TOTAL	Columns Above	
	Columns at Left	
	Total	

50

Net Income

	Husband	Wife	TOTAL
SALARY			
TOTAL INCOME			

Savings

(Describe)	
TOTAL SAVINGS	

Investments

(Describe)	
TOTAL INVESTMENTS	

Retirement

(Describe)	
TOTAL RETIREMENT	

	Food		Household			Transportation			Personal		Recreation		
	groceries	meals out	supplies, mainten	appliance furniture, furnishing	misc.	gas	auto mainten.	transit, tolls parking	clothing, sewing	health, beauty aids	vacation trips	entertain. clubs	hobbies lessons
1													
2													
3													
4													
5													
6													
7													
8													
9													
10													
11													
12													
13													
14													
15													
16													
17													
18													
19													
20													
21													
22													
23													
24													
25													
26													
27													
28													
29													
30													
31													
Total Spent													

June

Education		Miscellaneous			Tax Deductible Expenses					
tuition, supplies	books, maga-zines	gifts, cards	other	other	interest, taxes	medical	contri-butions	business education	childcare	explanation

	Fixed Expenses	
	MONTHLY	**AMOUNT**
1	Mortgage/ Rent	
2	Gas/Fuel	
3	Electricity	
4	Water	
5	Garbage	
6	Telephone	
7		
8		
9		
10	TOTAL	
11	**PERIODIC**	
12		
13	Insurance:	
14	House/Apt	
15	Auto	
16	Life	
17	Health	
18		
19	TOTAL	
20	**INSTALLMENT**	
21		
22	Loans/Credit Cards/etc.	
23		
24		
25		
26		
27		
28		
29		
30	TOTAL	
31	Columns Above	
GRAND TOTAL	Columns at Left	
	Total	

July 1986

52

Net Income

	Husband	Wife	TOTAL
SALARY	1479 81	2214 82	3694 63
TOTAL INCOME			

Savings

(Describe)	
EDUCATION FUND (MONIQUE)	50
EMERGENCY FUND (OPPENHEIMER)	225
TOTAL SAVINGS	

Investments

(Describe)	
TOTAL INVESTMENTS	

Retirement

(Describe)	
TOTAL RETIREMENT	

	Food		Household			Transportation			Personal		Recreation		
	groceries	meals out	supplies, mainten	appliance furniture, furnishing	misc.	gas	auto mainten.	transit, tolls parking	clothing, sewing	health, beauty aids	vacation trips	entertain. clubs	hobbie lesson
1						48.81			36.				
2	87.89												
3													
4													
5													
6						20.50							
7													
8													
9													
10													
11													
12													
13													
14													
15													
16													
17													
18													
19													
20													
21													
22													
23													
24													
25													
26													
27													
28													
29												7.50	
30													
31													
Total Spent													

Education		Miscellaneous			Tax Deductible Expenses					
tuition, supplies	books, maga-zines	gifts, cards	other	other (CASH)	interest, taxes	medical	contri-butions	business education	childcare	explanation
	44.52									
	25.20									
			20						60	
			5						20	
						77.50				

Fixed Expenses

	MONTHLY		AMOUNT
1	Mortgage/ Rent		1519 97
2	Gas/Fuel		
3	Electricity		
4	Water		
5	Garbage		
6	Telephone		
7	CHURCH (25+		
8	SVD CATV		25 24
9	RENTAL		800 —
10		TOTAL	

	PERIODIC		
11			
12			
13	Insurance:		
14	House/Apt		
15	Auto	(BMW DMV)	101
16	Life		
17	Health		
18			
19		TOTAL	

	INSTALLMENT		
20			
21			
22	Loans/Credit Cards/etc.		
23	B of A VISA		61
24	HOME FED. VISA		779 60
25	SEC. PAC. MNEY CNTR		104 03
26			
27			
28			
29			
30		TOTAL	
31	GRAND TOTAL	Columns Above	
		Columns at Left	
		Total	

54

Net Income

	Husband	Wife	TOTAL
SALARY			
TOTAL INCOME			

Savings

(Describe)	
TOTAL SAVINGS	

Investments

(Describe)	
TOTAL INVESTMENTS	

Retirement

(Describe)	
TOTAL RETIREMENT	

	Food		Household			Transportation			Personal		Recreation		
	groceries	meals out	supplies, mainten	appliance furniture, furnishing	misc.	gas	auto mainten.	transit, tolls parking	clothing, sewing	health, beauty aids	vacation trips	entertain. clubs	hobbi lesso
1													
2													
3													
4													
5													
6													
7													
8													
9													
10													
11													
12													
13													
14													
15													
16													
17													
18													
19													
20													
21													
22													
23													
24													
25													
26													
27													
28													
29													
30													
31													
Total Spent													

August

Education		Miscellaneous			Tax Deductible Expenses					
tuition, supplies	books, maga-zines	gifts, cards	other	other	interest, taxes	medical	contri-butions	business education	childcare	explanation

Fixed Expenses

	MONTHLY	AMOUNT
1	Mortgage/ Rent	
2	Gas/Fuel	
3	Electricity	
4	Water	
5	Garbage	
6	Telephone	
7		
8		
9		
10	TOTAL	
11	**PERIODIC**	
12		
13	Insurance:	
14	House/Apt	
15	Auto	
16	Life	
17	Health	
18		
19	TOTAL	
20	**INSTALLMENT**	
21		
22	Loans/Credit Cards/etc.	
23		
24		
25		
26		
27		
28		
29		
30	TOTAL	
31		
	GRAND TOTAL — Columns Above / Columns at Left	
	Total	

55

56

Net Income

	Husband	Wife	TOTAL
SALARY			
TOTAL INCOME			

Savings

(Describe)	
TOTAL SAVINGS	

Investments

(Describe)	
TOTAL INVESTMENTS	

Retirement

(Describe)	
TOTAL RETIREMENT	

	Food		Household			Transportation			Personal		Recreation		
	groceries	meals out	supplies, mainten	appliance furniture, furnishing	misc.	gas	auto mainten.	transit, tolls parking	clothing, sewing	health, beauty aids	vacation trips	entertain. clubs	hobbi lesso
1													
2													
3													
4													
5													
6													
7													
8													
9													
10													
11													
12													
13													
14													
15													
16													
17													
18													
19													
20													
21													
22													
23													
24													
25													
26													
27													
28													
29													
30													
31													
Total Spent													

September

57

Education		Miscellaneous			Tax Deductible Expenses					
tion, plies	books, maga- zines	gifts, cards	other	other	interest, taxes	medical	contri- butions	business education	childcare	explanation

Fixed Expenses

	MONTHLY	AMOUNT
1	Mortgage/ Rent	
2	Gas/Fuel	
3	Electricity	
4	Water	
5	Garbage	
6	Telephone	
7		
8		
9		
10	TOTAL	
11	**PERIODIC**	
12		
13	Insurance:	
14	House/Apt	
15	Auto	
16	Life	
17	Health	
18		
19	TOTAL	
20	**INSTALLMENT**	
21		
22	Loans/Credit Cards/etc.	
23		
24		
25		
26		
27		
28		
29		
30	TOTAL	
31		

GRAND TOTAL	Columns Above	
	Columns at Left	
	Total	

58

		Net Income					Food		Household			Transportation			Personal		Recreation		
		Husband	Wife	TOTAL			groceries	meals out	supplies, mainten	appliance furniture, furnishing	misc.	gas	auto mainten.	transit, tolls parking	clothing, sewing	health, beauty aids	vacation trips	entertain. clubs	hobbi lesson
SALARY					1														
					2														
					3														
					4														
					5														
					6														
					7														
					8														
					9														
					10														
TOTAL INCOME					11														
					12														
Savings					13														
(Describe)					14														
					15														
					16														
					17														
					18														
					19														
					20														
TOTAL SAVINGS					21														
					22														
Investments					23														
(Describe)					24														
					25														
					26														
TOTAL INVESTMENTS					27														
					28														
Retirement					29														
(Describe)					30														
					31														
TOTAL RETIREMENT					Total Spent														

October

Education		Miscellaneous			Tax Deductible Expenses					
tuition, supplies	books, maga-zines	gifts, cards	other	other	interest, taxes	medical	contri-butions	business education	childcare	explanation

Fixed Expenses

	MONTHLY	AMOUNT
1	Mortgage/ Rent	
2	Gas/Fuel	
3	Electricity	
4	Water	
5	Garbage	
6	Telephone	
7		
8		
9		
10	TOTAL	

	PERIODIC	
11		
12		
13	Insurance:	
14	House/Apt	
15	Auto	
16	Life	
17	Health	
18		
19	TOTAL	

	INSTALLMENT	
20		
21		
22	Loans/Credit Cards/etc.	
23		
24		
25		
26		
27		
28		
29		
30	TOTAL	

GRAND TOTAL	Columns Above	
	Columns at Left	
	Total	

59

60

Net Income

	Husband	Wife	TOTAL
SALARY			
TOTAL INCOME			

Savings

(Describe)	
TOTAL SAVINGS	

Investments

(Describe)	
TOTAL INVESTMENTS	

Retirement

(Describe)	
TOTAL RETIREMENT	

	Food		Household			Transportation			Personal		Recreation		
	groceries	meals out	supplies, mainten	appliance furniture, furnishing	misc.	gas	auto mainten.	transit, tolls parking	clothing, sewing	health, beauty aids	vacation trips	entertain. clubs	hobbies lessons
1													
2													
3													
4													
5													
6													
7													
8													
9													
10													
11													
12													
13													
14													
15													
16													
17													
18													
19													
20													
21													
22													
23													
24													
25													
26													
27													
28													
29													
30													
31													
Total Spent													

November

Left Table

Education		Miscellaneous			Tax Deductible Expenses					
tuition, supplies	books, magazines	gifts, cards	other	other	interest, taxes	medical	contributions	business education	childcare	explanation

Fixed Expenses

MONTHLY	AMOUNT
Mortgage/ Rent	
Gas/Fuel	
Electricity	
Water	
Garbage	
Telephone	
TOTAL	

PERIODIC	
Insurance:	
House/Apt	
Auto	
Life	
Health	
TOTAL	

INSTALLMENT	
Loans/Credit Cards/etc.	
TOTAL	

GRAND TOTAL	Columns Above	
	Columns at Left	
	Total	

61

62

Net Income

	Husband	Wife	TOTAL
SALARY			
TOTAL INCOME			

Savings

(Describe)	
TOTAL SAVINGS	

Investments

(Describe)	
TOTAL INVESTMENTS	

Retirement

(Describe)	
TOTAL RETIREMENT	

	Food		**Household**			**Transportation**			**Personal**		**Recreation**		
	groceries	meals out	supplies, mainten	appliance, furniture, furnishing	misc.	gas	auto mainten.	transit, tolls parking	clothing, sewing	health, beauty aids	vacation trips	entertain. clubs	hobbies lessons
1													
2													
3													
4													
5													
6													
7													
8													
9													
10													
11													
12													
13													
14													
15													
16													
17													
18													
19													
20													
21													
22													
23													
24													
25													
26													
27													
28													
29													
30													
31													
Total Spent													

December

63

Education		Miscellaneous			Tax Deductible Expenses					explanation
tuition, supplies	books, maga-zines	gifts, cards	other	other	interest, taxes	medical	contri-butions	business education	childcare	explanation

Fixed Expenses

	MONTHLY	AMOUNT
1	Mortgage/ Rent	
2	Gas/Fuel	
3	Electricity	
4	Water	
5	Garbage	
6	Telephone	
7		
8		
9		
10	TOTAL	
11	PERIODIC	
12		
13	Insurance:	
14	House/Apt	
15	Auto	
16	Life	
17	Health	
18		
19	TOTAL	
20	INSTALLMENT	
21		
22	Loans/Credit Cards/etc.	
23		
24		
25		
26		
27		
28		
29		
30	TOTAL	
31		

GRAND TOTAL	Columns Above	
	Columns at Left	
	Total	

	Net Income	Savings			Food		Household			Transportation			Personal		Recreation		
	net income	savings	invest-ments	retirement	groceries	meals out	supplies, maint.	appliance, furniture, furnishing	misc.	gas	auto maint.	transit, tolls parking	clothing, sewing	health, beauty aids	vacation, trips	entertain. clubs	hobbie lessor
JAN.																	
FEB.																	
MAR.																	
APR.																	
MAY																	
JUNE																	
JULY																	
AUG.																	
SEPT.																	
OCT.																	
NOV.																	
DEC.																	
Total																	
Mo. Ave.																	

64

Education		Misc.		Tax Deductible Expenses					Home	Utilities					Insur-ance	Install-ment	Total
tion, pplies	books, magazines	gifts, cards	other / other	interest, taxes	medical	contri-butions	business or educ.	childcare	mortgage rent	gas/fuel	electric	water	garbage	telephone	home auto life health		Monthly Expenses

65

	JAN.	FEB.	MAR.	APR.	MAY	JUNE	JULY	AUG.	SEPT.	OCT.	NOV.	DEC.	Total
Gross Income													
Federal													
State													
FICA													
Total													

66

		Medical and Dental Expenses					Medicine and Drugs		
DATE	MILEAGE	TO WHOM PAID	AMOUNT	INSUR. REIMBURS.	DATE	MILEAGE	TO WHOM PAID	AMOUNT	INSUR. REIMBU
Total					**Total**				
		Total Amount Paid					Total Amount Paid		
		Total Reimbursed					Total Reimbursed		
		Total Medical Cost					**Total Medical Cost**		

DATE	TO WHOM PAID-SERVICE	AMOUNT	DATE	TO WHOM PAID-SERVICE	AMOUNT	DATE	TO WHOM PAID-SERVICE	AMOUNT
	Total			Total			Total	

67

MISCELLANEOUS EXPENSE RECORD

DATE	TO WHOM PAID-SERVICE	AMOUNT	DATE	TO WHOM PAID-SERVICE	AMOUNT	DATE	TO WHOM PAID-SERVICE	AMOUN
	Total			Total			Total	

YOUR INVESTMENT PICTURE

If you followed the suggestions and guidelines in this workbook you probably already have or will soon have some basic savings and investments.

Whether you have money in company savings plans at work, inherited some bonds, invested in mutual funds, started changing your savings from passbooks to higher yielding C.D.s or money markets, or opened an IRA, it is important to keep records and know what you have.

Like personal finances, if you don't pay attention to your investments or keep careful records of them they can easily get away from you. Soon it's hard to remember just exactly where you put those IRA's purchased sometime in 1983 and 1984. What rate are they getting? What's the maturity date?

Or maybe through your parents or a divorce, you acquired some stocks which are just "sitting" in an account and you really don't know what you have. In today's fast-paced lifestyle, it is easy to leave the responsibility of knowing what you own to someone else — a banker, a broker, or an accountant, but by doing so, you sacrifice an understanding and awareness of your total financial picture.

The Investment/Savings Record chart provides a place for recording key information of your various investments. If you anticipate frequent changes, complete the form in pencil. The space on the right of the chart allows for a periodic follow-up of your current yield. The headings are used as a guildeline. If necessary, change them to be appropriate for your Investments. The important point is to be sure you have recorded all the information for each of your investments and have it all in one convenient place.

RESERVE FUND

In this section include records of liquid assets — money you can immediately get your hands on without withdrawal penalty — such as savings in your bank, credit union or money markets. These short-term savings are generally accumulated through direct deposit or money put into savings accounts, money markets or even a sock under the mattress (*not* an advisable holding place!).

Your savings for upcoming taxes and insurance or for unexpected emergencies (furnace or car break-down, for example) would be recorded in this section. Also included would be your savings for immediate or short-range goals, your Christmas savings, etc.

RETIREMENT

Record your retirement savings programs here. These range from savings funded and/or established by your employer, to personal IRA's, Keoghs, company pensions, and other tax sheltered investments.

A wide variety of employee retirement programs are offered through schools, hospitals, government and private firms. It is easy to forget or ignore these funds since they are often only shown as a paycheck deduction. Pay attention to and gather up the necessary information as outlined in this section so you are familiar with your current and past retirement programs.

SHORT/LONG TERM HOLDINGS

List investments held for short or extended periods to gain the maximum return. Some of these investments, such as CD's, T-Bills, bonds, etc., will have a fixed rate or time period and this information should be noted on the chart. Other securities (stocks, mutual funds, options) may change yields, time frames, and prices daily. This information should also be noted.

If you frequently buy, sell, and actively get involved with your investments, you may already have an investment portfolio with all the necessary information. On the other hand, if you do not do much with your investments, especially securities, *the information on this chart will be extremely helpful for tax, loan, or net worth purposes.*

OTHER

Your investments, such as real estate (other than personal residence), collectibles, trusts, limited or general partnerships, etc., would be recorded here. However, if the majority of those other investments are quite extensive you probably have them recorded through another system. If so, indicate here where you have those records and those of any of your other investments listed on this chart.

MAINTAINING CONTROL OF YOUR FINANCES

As you gather up your investment information you may find you need to develop your own follow-up system for those long range investments with maturity dates. Start a file and keep a copy of these worksheets for each year. Highlight the maturity dates so you have a quick reference.

These worksheets along with the others you have used in this workbook will help you to have all your financial information in one place, thus staying organized and aware of your finances!

RESERVE FUNDS	Name of Institution	Type	Account #	Date Opened	Amount Invested	Interest Rate	Owned By (husband, wife, joint)

RETIREMENT ACCOUNTS	Where Held	Type & Name	Account #	Purchase Date	Amount Invested	Interest Rate	Maturity Date

SHORT/LONG TERM HOLDINGS	Where Held	Type & Name	Certificate/ Account #	Purchase Date	Amount Invested	# of Shares	Unit Price	Dividend/ Interest Rate

OTHER	Location/Name	Date Purchased	Cost	Monthly/Yearly Income	Location of Records

CONTACT Name/Phone	LOCATION OF RECORDS	FOLLOW UP INFORMATION (date, balance, current yield)

Owned By (husband, wife, joint)	Contact Name/Phone	Location of Records	Date Sold	Net Proceeds	Gain/ Loss	Additional Notes

Date/Amount Dividend Paid	Maturity Date	Owned By (husband, wife, joint)	Contact Name/Phone	Location of Records	Date Sold	# Shares Sold	Net Proceeds	Gain/ Loss

Additional Notes (date sold, total proceeds, etc.)

An important step in gaining financial control is to take an ac-
counting of what your total financial worth is. Every year your
net worth should be tabulated to enable you to review your
progress and compare it with your financial goals. In addition,
a Net Worth Statement is a valuable aid in planning your
estate and establishing a record for loan and insurance purposes.

Date ________________

Assets

Cash: On Hand __________________
Checking Acct. __________________
Savings Accts __________________

Loans Receivable __________________

Cash Value
Life Insurance __________________

Real Estate (Present __________________
value, less sales
expense)
Home __________________
Other __________________

Investments: (Market __________________
Value)
Stocks __________________
Bonds __________________
Cert. of Deposits __________________
Other __________________
____

Personal Property:
(Present Value)
Home Furnishings __________________
Appliance __________________
Clothing __________________
Jewelry __________________
Automobiles __________________
Other __________________
____
____
____

Liabilities

Current Debts:
Household __________________
Credit Cards __________________
Insurance __________________
Taxes __________________
Other __________________

Mortgage on __________________
Real Estate:
Home __________________
Other __________________
Loans:
Bank __________________
Automobiles __________________
Household __________________
Other __________________

Other Debts __________________
____
____
____
____

Total Liabilities __________________

Total Assets __________________   Total Assets minus Total Liabilities = **Net Worth** __________________

KEEPING RECORDS

After a divorce it is so easy for depression, anger, fear, and loneliness to interfere with practical thoughts and actions.

During this time credit problems often crop up. This is not because you are incapable of managing your money, but often because you suddenly are overwhelmed with handling all the aspects of family life and household maintenance. Due dates, bills, and paper work may just seem to get away from you.

Keeping proper records of child support payments, children's expenses, and pertinent custody information is extremely important. However, with demands of trying to meet the physical and emotional needs of your children and yourself, these records are often neglected and never established.

The following charts were designed to help remove some of the burden of keeping important records. The charts give you guidelines to help you remember what records you should keep and provide you with a tool for having all your necessary information and records in one place. By organizing and controlling this aspect of your life you will be better equipped to move on to other pressing issues facing you every day.

If you are the noncustodial parent making the child support payments, recording the information called for can be just as important for you. If you need to prove what amount and when a support payment was actually made, received and cashed, or need to prove other significant information for tax or legal purposes, you will have the necessary records.

Utilize and modify the charts in this book so you can record information unique to your needs. For example, you may want to use the Medical and Dental Expense section for keeping detailed records of who paid a medical expense, the insurance deductible, or the difference not paid by insurance.

When using these charts, be aware that the state and federal laws and regulations vary. *The charts and text are not a substitute for legal advice from your local attorney. Consult with your attorney for any questions in this section.*

76

CHILD SUPPORT PAYMENT RECORD CHART

(1) These records are critical when you need help from your local enforcement agency because of late, short, or missing payments. The "Amount Due" column is for the monthly child support payment as ordered. Enter the amount received under *the month it arrives*, not for the month it was due. If no payment was received that month, note that under "Amount Received". Since these (2) payments may vary from once a week, or once a month, to sporadically for the year, you will have to modify this column to fit your needs.

(3) Record the other related child support obligations as ordered by the Divorce Decree such as medical insurance premium, unreimbursed medical expense, tuition, dues etc. Keep a copy of your Decree stating the terms, payment, custody, visitation and conditions of support in the pocket in the back of the book.

(4) Note under "Additional Information" if an item was substituted in lieu of a child support payment. Be sure to check with your attorney if this is an *acceptable form of child support*. If you do not wish to accept an item in lieu of a payment, ask your attorney if written notice should be given. If so, be sure to keep a copy.

(5) When recording the institution, number and date of the check or money order, use the symbols shown to indicate how the payment was made. If possible, keep a copy of all checks, money orders and envelopes. These copies will be helpful if a court or social agency ever needs to review your records in the event of a mishandling of child support, an excessive lag between the date of the check and the date it was sent, or a payment stopped on a check or money order you received. Keep these records in the pockets in the back of the book. Be sure to note if you are unable to make a copy of the checks, money order or envelopes (perhaps a check mark in front of the amount received).

You will find that this chart will contain some of your most important records. Stay with it.

Month	① Amount Due	② Amount Received	Amt. Past Due	⑤ # on: x-$ Order ✓-Check $-Cash	Date on: x-$ order ✓-Check $-Cash	Date Payment Received	⑤ Institution and Account Number	③ Other Expenses*	④ Additional Information/Action Taken (check status, gifts etc.)
JAN									
FEB									
MAR									
APR									
MAY									
JUNE									
JULY									
AUG									
SEPT									
OCT									
NOV									
DEC									
Total									

*Stipulated by Decree

THE COST OF RAISING CHILDREN

If you need or want to analyze the cost of raising your children, to show the use of support provided or to demonstrate the need for increased support, use the Monthly Expense Record section.

Enter all your children's daily expenses along with all your other expenses on the Monthly Expense Record pages. Modify the headings to fit your individual needs. Use a highlighter, colored pencil or check mark to show which expenses are the children's. Total the children's expenses in the columns that apply and record the total at the bottom of the page below the family total. If you have a question about allocating expenses shared by you and your children, ask your local attorney.

Another method used by some families for keeping accurate records is a separate checking account used strictly for children's expenses. Use the method that works best for you.

If you save all your receipts in envelopes labeled for the different categories, you can file these in the pockets in the back of this book.

CHILD SUPPORT ENFORCEMENT & CHILD VISITATION RECORDS

In 1984 Congress passed the "Child Support Enforcement Amendments of 1984" which strengthens the child support enforcement laws throughout the country. The information you record will bo invaluable if you over need the services of a Child Support Enforcement Bureau in your state to help you collect past due child support.

If you would like more information about Child Support Enforcement write the Consumer Information Center, Dept. 628 M, Pueblo, CO, 81009 and ask for a free copy of "Kids, They're Worth Every Penny: Handbook on Child Support Enforcement" put out by the Office of Child Support Enforcement in Washington D.C.

REDUCED ANXIETY

These charts can't take away the pain. They can, however, help reduce some of the anxiety associated with the aftermath of a divorce. As you start taking charge of your situation and gain new knowledge you will regain self confidence and self esteem in the process.

BEST OF LUCK TO YOU!

NON CUSTODIAL PARENT:

Full Name	Social Security Number	Birth Date / Place	Height	Weight	Occupation

Last Known Address(s)			Address Dates	Home Telephone

Last Known Employer(s)	Address		Address Dates	Work Telephone

Child Support Enforcement Office	Telephone Number	Case Worker's Name / Phone	Case Number	Court Order No.

79

Note: Get a Birth Registration Card from your Vital Statistics
Office. This will have all your children's information
printed on it so you will have the information handy.

CHILD VISITATION RECORD

MONTH	JAN	FEB	MAR	APR	MAY	JUNE	JULY	AUG	SEPT	OCT	NOV	DEC
DATES OF VISITATION												

NOTES

80

NOTES

NOTES

NOTES

NOTES